KT-226-039

MATERIALS THAT MATTER

PAPER

Neil Morris

W

FRANKLIN WATTS

LONDON • SYDNEY

An Appleseed Editions book

First published in 2010 by Franklin Watts
338 Euston Road, London NW1 3BH

Franklin Watts Australia
Hachette Children's Books
Level 17/207 Kent St, Sydney, NSW 2000

© 2010 Appleseed Editions

Created by Appleseed Editions Ltd,
Well House, Friars Hill, Guestling,
East Sussex TN35 4ET

Designed by Helen James
Edited by Mary-Jane Wilkins
Artwork by Graham Rosewarne
Picture research by Su Alexander

All rights reserved. No part of this publication may be reproduced,
stored in a retrieval system or transmitted in any form or by any means,
electronic, mechanical, photocopying, recording or otherwise, without
prior permission of the publisher.

ISBN 978 1 4451 0022 7

Dewey Classification: 620.1'97

A CIP catalogue for this book is available from the British Library.

Photograph acknowledgements
page 4 Neil Holmes Freelance Digital/Alamy; 5 Bill Barksdale/AgStock Images/Corbis;
6 INTERPHOTO/Alamy; 7 British Library/AKG; 8 Bettmann/Corbis; 9 Christopher Taylor/
Alamy; 10 Bill Brooks/Alamy; 11 Paul Almasy/Corbis; 12 Richard Bickel/Corbis; 13 David R Frazier
Photolibrary, Inc./Alamy; 14 Edward Parker/Alamy; 16 Robert Essel NYC/Corbis; 17 Eric Fowke/
Alamy; 18 ImageState/Alamy; 19 Coffeehouse Productions/Alamy; 20 British Library/The Art Archive;
21 epa/Corbis; 22 Walter Hodges/Corbis; 24 Gabe Palmer/Corbis; 25 Jose Luis Pelaez, Inc./Corbis;
26 Anna Clopet/Corbis; 27 Lester Lefkowitz/Corbis; 28 Enigma/Alamy; 29 Paolo Negri/Alamy
Front cover Robert Essel NYC/Corbis

Printed in China

Franklin Watts is a division of Hachette Children's Books,
an Hachette UK company.
www.hachette.co.uk

Contents

What is paper?

We all know what paper looks like. The pages of this book are made of paper, and so is the book's cover. If we give someone a book as a present, we might put it in colourful wrapping paper. Many other things are made of paper, including newspapers, magazines, writing pads, birthday cards and toilet rolls.

This supermarket sells a wide range of magazines on all sorts of subjects. Magazines, books and newspapers are all made of paper.

All paper is made of millions of tiny **fibres**. These fibres are made of a plant substance called **cellulose**. We make paper by mixing cellulose fibres with water and turning them into a sheet that dries to form paper.

Small cells

The word cellulose comes from the French *cellule*, meaning small cell. Scientists call cellulose a **carbohydrate**, which means that it is made up of **carbon**, **hydrogen** and **oxygen**. Sugar and starch are also carbohydrates.

Cellulose forms the main part of the cell walls of plants, including trees and grasses. It makes up about a third of all vegetable matter, but the exact amount varies from plant to plant. For example, cellulose makes up half of wood and nine tenths of cotton. Cellulose fibres are tiny: about 0.1 mm wide and 1.3 mm long.

USE IT AGAIN AND AGAIN

All kinds of paper can be used again and again (see pages 24-27 on recycling). It is impossible to tell whether a book or newspaper is made from new or recycled paper. When we recycle paper we help the environment. Every time we recycle a tonne of paper:

• we use 3000-4000 kWh (**kilowatt hours**) less electricity than when making new paper (enough to power an average house for a year);

• we use 30,000 fewer litres of water;

• we create 95% less air **pollution**.

Hard and soft wood

The cellulose fibres used to make paper come mostly from trees. About three quarters of papermaking wood comes from **softwood** trees. Many are specially grown for this, but paper manufacturers also use

TREES FOR MAKING PAPER

softwood	hardwood
fir	acacia
pine	aspen
spruce	birch
Western hemlock	eucalyptus
	maple
	oak
	poplar

offcuts and trimmings from trees that are cut down to make timber for furniture and other things. Any unwanted wood is turned into wood chips that are then pulped (see pages 12-13). Softwood comes from **coniferous** (cone-bearing, needle-leaved) trees such as spruce. The long fibres (2-4 mm) make strong paper. **Hardwood** comes from broadleaved trees, such as birch. It has shorter fibres (0.5-1.5 mm) and generally makes smoother paper.

Loggers chop down trees for building material as well as to make paper. These logs are being loaded on to a truck in a forest in Mississippi, USA.

The first paper

The word paper comes from papyrus, a reed which the ancient Egyptians used to make writing material. They cut papyrus stems into narrow strips and pressed them together into sheets, which they could then roll up. The sheets and rolls are also called papyri, and the oldest surviving examples are more than 5000 years old.

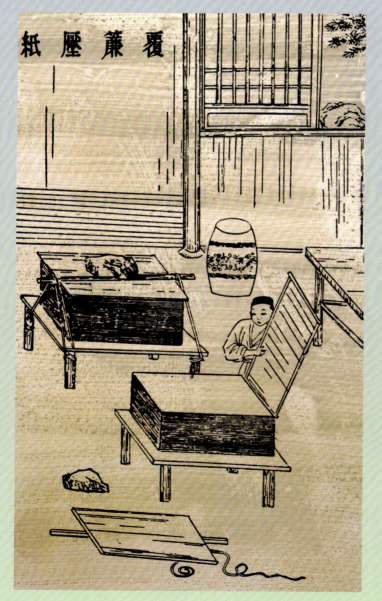

Other ancient peoples used wood or bark for carving inscriptions. The word book comes from the Old English term *boc*, meaning beech tree. The first real paper was invented 2000 years ago in ancient China.

The story of Cai Lun

A traditional Chinese story tells how a court official named Cai Lun (c.AD 50-121) invented paper. Some historians believe that the first paper was actually made a few hundred years earlier and that Cai Lun just improved the way it was done. He belonged to the court of Emperor He (79-105) of the Eastern Han dynasty and was unhappy with the writing materials that were available. Bamboo was heavy and silk (another Chinese invention)

This eighteenth-century illustration shows the ancient Chinese method of making paper in wooden frames. Chinese craftsmen perfected their technique over centuries.

CHINESE PAPER

Cai Lun used the sides of a wooden box as a frame or **mould**. He fitted a screen into the box. This was probably made of woven cloth, and was replaced by later papermakers with strips of bamboo. Cai Lun added water to make a slushy **pulp** from the bark and other ingredients. He poured the pulp on to the screen, stirred the solution and then lifted the screen out of the frame, with a thin layer of wet pulp attached. He dried this in the sun for several hours, and it turned into a sheet of paper.

was precious and expensive. In 105 Cai Lun made paper by soaking various materials together in water. These included mulberry tree bark, stems of the **hemp** plant, old pieces of cloth (or silk) and fishing net rope. He then drained the water and let the material dry into a thin sheet of paper.

From Asia to Europe

The ancient Chinese realized how important their invention was and they tried to keep it secret. This proved impossible though, and the technique had reached ancient Korea by the seventh century. It was then taken to Japan by **Buddhist** priests. In 751, the Chinese lost the Battle of Talas (in modern Kyrgyzstan) to the Arabs,

and Chinese prisoners of war were forced to share their knowledge of papermaking.

By 793 there was a paper mill in the city of Baghdad (in modern Iraq). Papermaking had spread to Damascus (in modern Syria) by the time of the first **crusade** in 1096. European Christian knights then took the knowledge back to Europe, and the Moors also introduced the technology when they conquered Spain. By the fourteenth century mills were producing paper in Spain, France, Germany and Italy.

This nineteenth-century illustration shows workers in an early Persian paper mill.

Discoveries and inventions

From the 1400s there were many new inventions in papermaking. Johannes Gutenberg (c.1400-68) printed a version of the Bible in Mainz, Germany, in 1455. Gutenberg printed 180 copies – 135 on paper and 45 on vellum (parchment made from calfskin). Later that century papermaking spread to England.

The first paper mill in the United States was built in Philadelphia in 1690. Papermaking changed dramatically in the middle of the nineteenth century, when new steam-powered machines started turning out six times as much paper as hand-operated mills.

Johannes Gutenberg checks a page that has just come off his new printing press.

Learning from wasps

The French scientist René Antoine de Réaumur (1683-1757) learned a lot by studying insects. He noticed that wasps used a type of paper to build their nests. Female wasps first chewed tiny pieces of wood from trees or timber. They wet the wood with **saliva**, making a pulp for their papery nest. In the eighteenth century, papermakers still used mainly linen and cotton rags for the fibres to make pulp. Despite Réaumur's discovery, human papermakers did not start using wood pulp on a large scale until the middle of the nineteenth century. This happened when new machines started making large quantities of paper very quickly, and new forms of pulp were needed.

French machines

In 1798 the French inventor Nicholas Louis Robert (1761-1828) invented a machine that could produce paper in a long sheet. Nine years later, two English brothers, Henry (1766-1854) and Sealy Fourdrinier (1774-1847) built an improved version. The early machines left the paper wet at the end of

Paper is still made in the traditional way at a working water-powered mill in central France.

the process, so it had to be hung up to dry. Machine-makers soon added steam-driven drying rollers, so the paper was ready to use at the end of the process. The French inventor Marc Isambard Brunel (1769-1849) called the Fourdriniers' machine, 'one of the most splendid inventions of the age'.

More and more paper

The first Fourdrinier machine in the United States started working in 1827. The new technology produced a huge amount more paper: in 1810, 3000 tonnes of paper were made in the USA. Thirty years later, papermakers were making about ten times as much. By 1900, this had increased to two million tonnes.

SPEEDING UP

By the 1860s, improved Fourdrinier machines were turning out 30 metres of paper a minute. By 1900, the best machines were twice as fast. Later in the twentieth century, machines could produce more than 1500 metres of paper every minute.

Raw materials

The main raw material for today's paper is wood. Papermakers also use cellulose fibres from other woody plants, such as straw, sugar cane, esparto grass, bamboo, flax, hemp and jute. Today, high-quality writing and art papers are still made from cotton and linen fibres.

Years ago, wood arrived at the pulp or paper mill from a nearby forest as large logs. Tree trunks were taken to the mill by rail or road. Sometimes they were hauled to the nearest river and floated to the mill.

There the first job was to remove the bark, which contains fewer fibres than wood. Today, the bark is usually used as **biofuel** and is burned to generate steam and drive machinery. Modern mills use wood chips

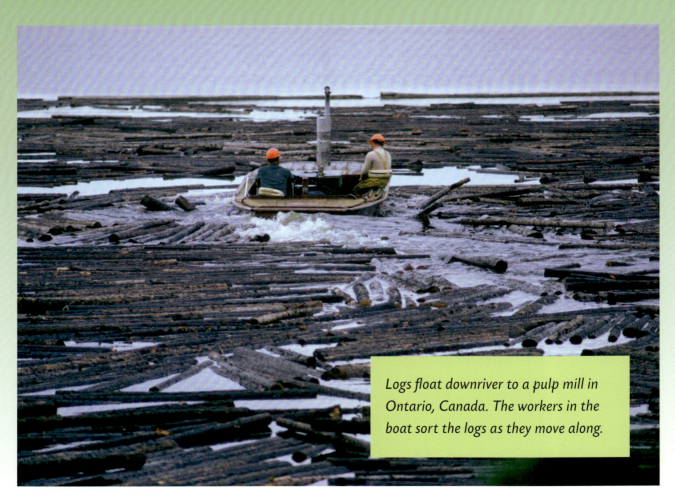

Logs float downriver to a pulp mill in Ontario, Canada. The workers in the boat sort the logs as they move along.

In this traditional French mill, huge wooden stampers (or hammers) pound wet rags for 36 hours to turn them into pulp for papermaking.

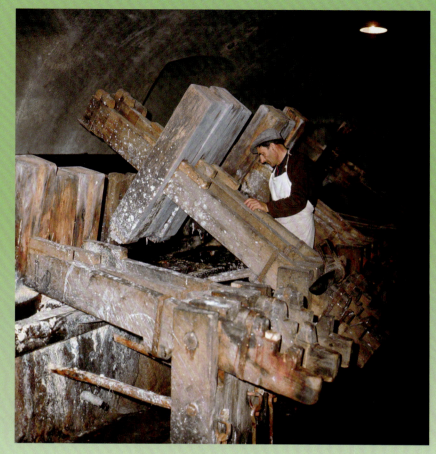

rather than logs. Wood-chipping machines with large, strong blades can reduce logs to small pieces just a few centimetres across.

Paper from rags

For centuries, the main raw materials used in papermaking were cotton and linen rags. They were often bought from a local rag merchant (or rag-and-bone man) and taken to a paper mill's rag house. There, workers took off buttons and other fasteners before sending the rags to the **beater house**, where they were beaten by water-powered **stampers**.

Papermakers still use clean rags to make papers which are especially strong and durable. These include bank notes, certificates, art paper and high-quality stationery. Today most of the rags we put in our recycling boxes are used in a different way. High-quality textiles are sent to developing countries to be used for clothes. Low-quality rags are shredded and used as mattress fillers or industrial cloths.

RENEWABLE RESOURCE

Trees are a renewable resource so long as forests are well managed. This means that foresters need to plant new trees to replace the ones they cut down and avoid cutting down too many trees at a time. An international organization called the Forest Stewardship Council (FSC) adds its logo to paper which is made from trees that are harvested in the least damaging way. The FSC controls more than 109 million **hectares** of forest around the world.

RECYCLE RECYCLE RECYCLE RECYCLE

Making pulp

Raw materials are turned into pulp for papermaking at a pulp mill. This may be part of a paper mill or a separate building on the same site. At the pulp mill the wood is turned to pulp in one of three different ways.

This large pulp mill in Florida, USA, pumps out steam and smoke as it turns wood to pulp.

The three ways of making pulp are mechanical, chemical and semi-chemical. All separate cellulose fibres from **lignin**, the natural substance that keeps the fibres together. Then the cellulose fibres are mixed with water to form a pulp.

Ground by machines

The first pulp mills ground wood against slabs of sandstone which were turned by

HOW MANY TREES?

You need about 13 trees – each about 12 metres tall – to produce one tonne of pulp by the mechanical process. You need about twice as many trees to make the same amount of pulp by the kraft process. The mechanical process uses a lot of electricity – about 10,000 **megajoules** to make one tonne of pulp.

This wood pulp has been bleached to make whiter paper.

water wheels. Today, the stones have been replaced by rotating steel discs, which grind wood chips against a fixed plate. The chips may be heated first, to make them easier to grind. Ground wood pulp produces paper that tends to go yellow as it get older. This is mainly used for newsprint, the low-quality paper on which newspapers are printed.

Using chemicals

Chemicals can dissolve the lignin that holds wood fibres together. To do this the chipped wood is heated in water with various chemicals. One method is called the **sulphate** (or kraft) process. This produces the most pulp around the world. The chemicals **sodium hydroxide** (caustic soda) and **sodium sulphide** cook the chips in a steam-heated tank called a **digester**. The chemical processes produce all sorts of different papers.

A partly-chemical process uses both methods. First the papermaker uses chemicals to soften the wood chips which a machine then grinds up. **Corrugated** cardboard and cheap printing paper is made in this way.

Bleaching

Papermakers **bleach** some pulps to produce whiter, brighter paper. The chemicals used can damage the environment, and many

pulp mills have changed the way they bleach so they do not pollute lakes or rivers. Some older pulp mills have closed to prevent pollution, such as the mill beside Lake Baikal, in Russia, the world's deepest lake.

PULP FICTION

Books have been recycled for centuries. In 1883, an article in the *Fortnightly Review* magazine said: 'Many unsaleable books are wasted, that is, are sent to the mill, ground up, pulped down, and made again into paper.' By 'wasted', the writer meant recycled. Cheap novels and magazines which were printed on low-quality paper were known as pulp magazines and pulp novels.

At the paper mill

The pulp that arrives at the paper mill is called stock. To prepare it for papermaking, it is beaten in a large mixing machine, which helps the fibres stick together. Sometimes starch or clay is added, depending on the type of paper being made. Then the pulp passes between turning blades in a machine called a refiner. This trims the fibres and makes them more flexible.

Once the pulp has been refined it may be mixed with other things to make special papers, or dye is added to make coloured paper. Then the stock is ready for the papermaking machine.

The wet stage

The papermaking machine mixes pulp and water and spreads it across a moving wire screen. The water drains through the vibrating wires, leaving a mat of fibres on the screen. Heavy rollers then squeeze more water from the wet mat and press it into

A fast, efficient machine produces large rolls of paper at a modern paper mill in Sweden.

Who makes the most?

The United States makes the most paper and wood pulp. China imports more wood pulp than it produces, but it also uses a lot of recycled paper. Canada exports nearly half the wood pulp it produces.

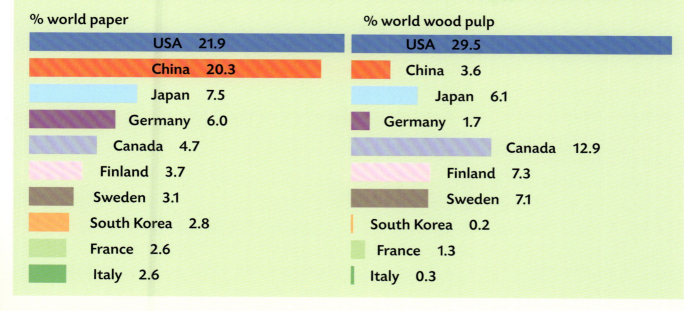

% world paper		% world wood pulp	
USA	21.9	USA	29.5
China	20.3	China	3.6
Japan	7.5	Japan	6.1
Germany	6.0	Germany	1.7
Canada	4.7	Canada	12.9
Finland	3.7	Finland	7.3
Sweden	3.1	Sweden	7.1
South Korea	2.8	South Korea	0.2
France	2.6	France	1.3
Italy	2.6	Italy	0.3

a smooth sheet. It goes through more rollers before moving to the drying section.

Drying and smoothing

The wet sheet goes through a series of steam-heated cylinders. Then more substances may be added. Coating the surface of the paper by adding **resins**, starches or chalks can make it more waterproof, stronger, shinier and better for printing. Finally, the sheet is smoothed by passing through a stack of rollers called calenders. The machine then winds the finished dry sheet on to large reels, ready to be sent to printers and other manufacturers.

Swedish papermaking

Papermaking has been important in Sweden for hundreds of years. The Holmen Paper company opened its first mill making handmade paper in 1633 in the town of Norrköping. Its first water-driven paper machine started in 1837. Today, the company has three machines in nearby Braviken, using spruce wood and recycled pulp. They produce 775,000 tonnes of 8.5-metre wide reels of newsprint a year.

LONG AND FAST

Paper machines can be 135 metres long from beginning to end reel. They can produce up to 1800 metres of paper per minute, which means that the whole papermaking cycle can take less than five seconds.

Many types of paper

Papermakers have different names for the types of paper they produce. There are also names and codes for different sizes and weights of paper. Large books such as dictionaries and bibles are printed on a thin book paper. Paper for printing needs a special finish, especially if colour illustrations are printed on it.

Bond and bank

Bond paper is high-quality business paper. It is strong and hard-wearing and used for printed letterheads (A4 paper with a printed name on top) and letters. It may be different colours, such as grey or beige. White bond is used in computer printers. Bank paper is similar, but much thinner (less than 50 gsm).

Coated papers

Coating gives paper a smooth finish for printing – gloss, matt, satin or silk. The finish on machine-coated papers is put on by the paper machine (see page 15). Off-machine coating is put on by separate machines immediately after the paper is made. Glossy paper goes through an extra series of rollers called a supercalender. This is good for printing books and magazines in colour.

A worker checks the finished paper's quality in an American mill.

The watermark of an American $20 bill shows the face of Andrew Jackson (1767-1845), the seventh president of the United States.

Watermarks

A watermark is a faint pattern you see when you hold paper up to the light. High-quality writing papers have a watermark which might show the brand or name of the maker.

Bank notes and certificates sometimes use a face as a watermark, which shows that the note is genuine. The mark is made by a pattern of wires on a roller in the papermaking machine.

WHAT DOES PAPER WEIGH?

The weight of paper is usually written in grams per square metre or gsm. Most ordinary office or copy paper weighs 80 gsm. This means that a single A4 sheet (which covers $1/16$ of a square metre) weighs 5g.

THE PAPER IN THIS BOOK

The paper this book is printed on was made in Ohio, USA. The name of the paper is Mead Anthem and it weighs 118 gsm.

International paper sizes

The most common size of paper is A4, which measures 210 mm across and 297 mm down. Most paper is sold in sizes ranging from A0 to A7 and all the sizes are the same shape. A0 is the biggest and each size is exactly half the size of the previous one.

If you fold an A3 sheet in half you make two A4 sheets. A folded A4 sheet makes two A5 sheets. In the USA, basic letter paper is slightly different, measuring 216 x 279 mm.

Paper for packaging

Cardboard is simply thick paper, and it is also made on paper machines. You see cardboard everywhere, in packaging, as cartons and other containers and as backing for writing pads and envelopes.

Paperboard

Cardboard that is more than 0.25 mm thick is called paperboard. One type called boxboard is used to make boxes and cartons for food and household products. These range from breakfast cereals, toothpaste and washing-powder packets to cartons for milk or orange juice. The card can easily be printed, so the producers can advertise on their packets. Many supermarkets ask their food suppliers to make their packaging attractive, so more shoppers will buy their products.

Corrugated board

Have you noticed that some large boxes are made of more than one layer of cardboard?

Opposite: workers control and check production in a cardboard-box factory.

Corrugated board protects products when they are transported – it is strong enough to absorb knocks and stop the contents being damaged.

A corrugated container starts off as rolls of paperboard. Two boards are joined in the middle by a corrugated (wavy) board called a flute. This is made by a machine which pushes the flat board into ridges. The flute is glued inside the two boards, called liners, leaving air in the space between them. This acts as a **shock absorber**. The corrugated board is then cut into the right shape, before being folded and glued into a box.

You can see the wavy flutes inside these pieces of corrugated cardboard which are used to make boxes.

PAPER PRODUCTS

Lots of household products are made of paper. Here are just a few. You can probably think of many more.

coffee filters   disposable nappies
drinking straws   egg cartons
lampshades   paper plates and cups
paper towels   place mats
shoeboxes   tea bags
toilet rolls   wallpaper
coasters   beer mats

RECYCLE RECYCLE RECYCLE RECYCLE

RECYCLING PACKAGING

Environmentalists want us to use less packaging. Often packaging is there just to advertise a product and it creates a huge amount of waste paper. In some countries, such as Germany, supermarket customers are encouraged to unwrap goods at the checkout after they have paid for them. They can then leave the unwanted packaging at the store, where it is collected for reuse or recycling.

Books and bindings

Paper is ideal for writing, drawing and printing on. Printing can quickly produce thousands of copies of writing or drawings – every one the same. In past centuries, printing inks were pressed on to paper. Today, most books are printed by a process called lithography.

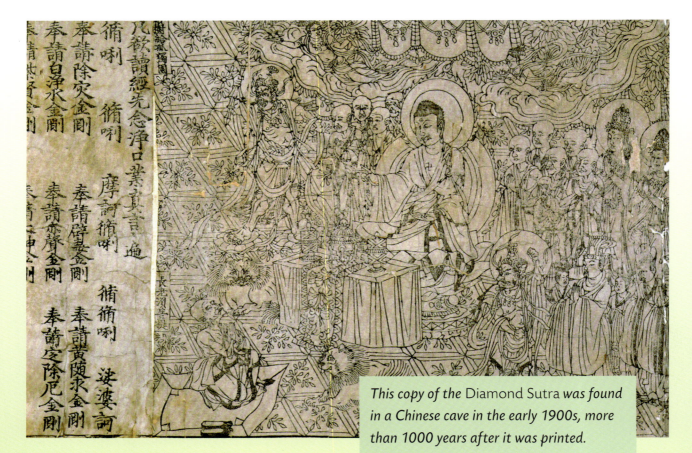

This copy of the Diamond Sutra *was found in a Chinese cave in the early 1900s, more than 1000 years after it was printed.*

Oil and water

In 1796 an Austrian playwright called Alois Senefelder (1771-1834) polished a flat piece of limestone and wrote and drew on it with a greasy crayon. Then he wet the stone with water before putting ink on it. The ink stuck only to the drawing and writing. When he pressed paper against the stone, his design was transferred to the paper. Senefelder had discovered the idea of lithography (which means 'stone writing').

Paper sheets

To make books, paper manufacturers cut rolls of paper into large sheets for printing.

FIRST PRINTED BOOK

The oldest printed book still in existence is probably the *Diamond Sutra*. This sacred Buddhist text was printed in China in 868 on paper made from mulberry bark using carved wooden blocks. The copy in the British Library in London has seven strips of paper pasted together to form a scroll more than five metres long. By the middle of the eleventh century, the Chinese were printing on paper with movable clay type. This meant that the letters which made up words could be moved around and reused.

An Indian printer checks the quality of political posters.

Each sheet is usually printed with 32 pages of the book (16 pages on either side). The printer puts a large stack of paper at one end of the printing press and the sheets travel through the machine as they are printed. Different colours are printed one at a time, until the sheet is complete.

Folding and binding

To finish a book, the printed sheets are fed into a folding machine. The pages are laid out on the large sheet so that they will be in the right order once the sheet is folded. Afterwards the paper is trimmed to make the pages the right size and to separate the pages. Finally a machine binds the pages inside the cover.

PAPER, PAPER EVERYWHERE

Just over a million new books are printed and published around the world every year. The UK publishes more books than any other country in the world (21 per cent of the total), followed by the US (17 per cent) and China (10 per cent).

Creating with paper

Many artists and designers create on paper, writing, drawing and painting in sketch pads or on large pieces of art paper. Other artists use paper as part of their artwork, folding and building with it, or make paper by hand.

Handmade paper

Specialist companies sell handmade paper, and some artists and designers make their own. They work in the same way as the ancient Chinese, using a mould and a **deckle**. A mould is a frame covered with a screen. The deckle is a flat metal frame which covers the mould and contains wet pulp. It leaves an irregular or feathery edge on the paper, called a deckle edge. Some manufacturers copy this effect to make their machine-made paper look handmade.

Japanese folding paper

Origami is the traditional Japanese art of folding paper into shapes. The word origami means 'folded paper' in Japanese. The traditional designs are often symbols of good luck such as cranes, lobsters or tortoises. Today, people also make paper toys or houses from folded paper. Traditionally, origami is done with a square piece of paper which is coloured on one side, without cutting or pasting the paper. You can use ordinary copy paper, but in

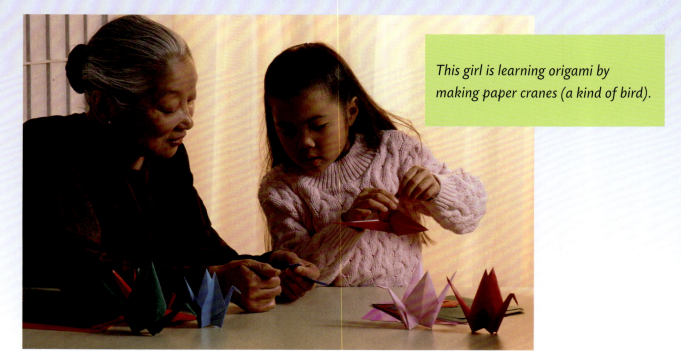

This girl is learning origami by making paper cranes (a kind of bird).

Alice is too big for Rabbit's house, in a pop-up picture from Robert Sabuda's Alice's Adventures in Wonderland. *Sabuda is an American artist and paper engineer.*

Japan they use handmade washi, which is often made from tree bark.

Paper creations

Artists make collages by sticking pieces of paper and other **found objects** on to a backing paper. A German artist named Kurt Schwitters (1887-1948) created pictures from paper objects such as bus tickets, postage stamps and pieces of newspaper. He became famous for his collage work, as well as for **graphic design** and **typography**. Many people have created similar works since, and some have even pretended that their works were done by Schwitters.

Paper engineering

Paper engineers are designers who create pop-ups and other mechanical books. These first became popular in the 1800s and many are printed today as novelty books for children. The books have tabs to pull, rings to turn, flaps to lift, and scenes that stand up from the page in three dimensions. Some use similar folding techniques to origami. The books are put together by hand, which makes them expensive to produce. The Movable Book Society, formed in 1993, shares knowledge between artists, collectors, designers and book producers.

USING WASTE

Pulp for handmade paper is usually made from **cotton** or **silk** waste. Sometimes waste from sugar cane or jute is used too.

23

Reduce, reuse, recycle

There are many reasons for using less paper. First, making paper uses a lot electricity. Most electricity is made by burning coal, oil or natural gas which puts waste gases into the Earth's atmosphere, causing pollution.

The pollution adds to the **greenhouse effect** and causes global warming. In the US pulp and paper mills are some of the worst polluters of air, water and land.

The three Rs

We can all help to waste less paper by putting the three Rs into action. The letters stand for:

- reduce
- reuse
- recycle.

LOOK FOR RECYCLED PAPER

Stationers and supermarkets sell paper which is labelled 'from recycled paper' – look out for this and buy it when you can. Recycled paper is not usually bleached, so the paper might not be as white or bright as completely new paper, but fewer chemicals are used to make it, which is better for the environment.

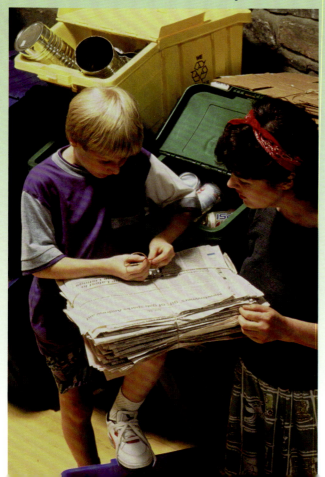

Reducing means cutting down on waste by using less in the first place. We could reduce waste by using less paper packaging (see pages 18-19) and we could also reuse more paper. We can draw, write or print on both sides of the paper we use. We could also fill the whole sheet before starting on another

It's easy to collect used and waste paper and put it in a recycling bin.

RECYCLE RECYCLE RECYCLE

NEWSPAPERS FOR MODEL MAKING

Have you ever made a model with papier mâché? If so, you recycled paper to make something new. You make papier mâché (which is French for 'chewed paper') from torn strips of old newspapers. First you soak the paper pieces in warm water to make pulp. Then mix it with wallpaper paste, glue, or flour and water to make a sticky mixture which can be shaped. As the papier mâché dries, it goes hard. Once it is dry you can paint it.

This boy is painting a model dinosaur made from papier mâché.

RECYCLE RECYCLE RECYCLE

one. Finally, instead of throwing paper away in the rubbish bin, we can put it in a recycling bin. Then, instead of being dumped in a landfill site, the old paper will be reused to make new paper.

Instead of trees

Another idea is to use more agricultural waste for making paper, rather than cutting down so many trees. This waste can be used to make something called agri-pulp. A company in Costa Rica specializes in making paper from the parts of banana, coffee and tobacco plants that are thrown away by other firms.

WOMBAT WASTE

On the Australian island of Tasmania, a company makes paper from the droppings of one of Australia's favourite animals – the wombat. The wombat is a marsupial (which means it has a pouch) and lives mainly in coastal forests, feeding on plants, bark and roots. Wombat dung contains a lot of fibre which can be used to make pulp. The paper is popular with tourists.

Recycling paper

Nearly half of all the paper we use has been recycled. Three kinds of scrap paper can be recycled. One is called mill broke – waste trimmings from paper mills. Another is called pre-consumer waste, which includes offcuts from printers, envelope trimmings and rejected papers and printings. The third type is called post-consumer waste, which is waste paper from offices and homes, old newspapers and packaging.

The third type of scrap paper makes up the largest proportion of recycled paper, and it is collected from homes by rubbish trucks or at neighbourhood recycling points.

Preparing and cleaning

Waste paper often has different types of paper made from various fibres, including office waste paper, old newspapers, card and board. These are sorted before they are turned back into pulp. Recycled paper pulp can be used to make paper of the same or lower quality. Papermakers can't make higher quality paper unless they mix it with new pulp.

String, strapping, paper clips, staples and other objects are removed from sorted

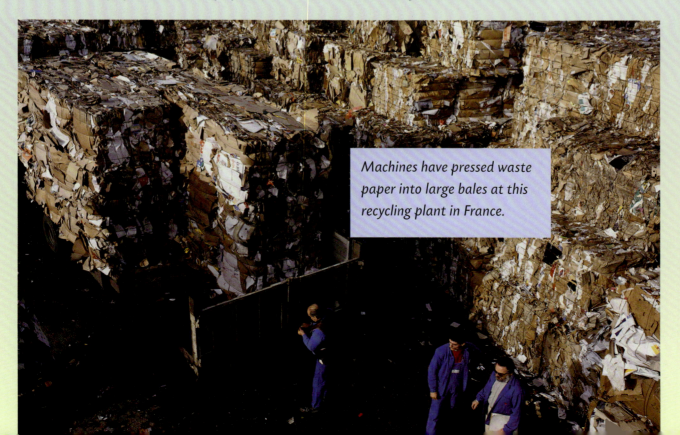

Machines have pressed waste paper into large bales at this recycling plant in France.

Mexico 2.2%

Spain 2.9%
Italy 2.9%
France 3.1%
South Korea 4.1%

UK 4.4%

Germany 8.1%

rest of the world 20.5%

USA 23.9%

China 16.1%

Japan 11.8%

Waste paper is separated and sorted, ready to be turned back into pulp.

WHO RECYCLES THE MOST?

About 43 per cent of all paper used around the world is recycled. The pie chart above shows the world's top producers of recycled paper. Together, the United States, China and Japan make up more than half of the world's recycled paper total.

RECYCLE RECYCLE RECYCLE RECYCLE

paper when bales arrive at a mill. A large magnet removes metal and as the paper is pulped, a set of turning wires called a ragger catches pieces of string. Some pulp mills also use a hooked tool called a junker to fish out other unwanted bits. Glue-based backing and binding materials are the most difficult to remove – these are called 'stickies'.

Washing off the ink

If ink spreads through recycled pulp it can give it a grey tinge. Pulpers wash off ink by putting the paper in water with chemicals which separate the ink from the paper. They rinse the fibres several times, draining off the water between rinses. Another method is to add chemicals to the pulp and blow air through it to make foam and form a sticky froth on top. The air bubbles take the ink to the surface where the froth is removed.

A paperless future?

For years people thought that we would use less paper as we use computers more, but this has not happened. Today we use more paper than ever before. Will this change? Banks, phone and fuel companies now send statements and bills direct to their customers' computers, so they use less paper and this may happen more in future.

Using paper

In the world's rich, developed countries, most people use about 152 kilograms of paper per year. This is 12 times more than people in developing countries, where people usually do not have enough paper. The countries which use most paper per person every year are Finland, the US, Canada, Belgium and Japan.

ENDLESS RECYCLING?

Today paper cannot generally be recycled more than six times because the fibres grow shorter and weaker every time they are pulped. New pulp has to be added to keep up the strength and quality of the fibres. Perhaps future scientists will find a way to overcome this so that paper can be recycled endlessly.

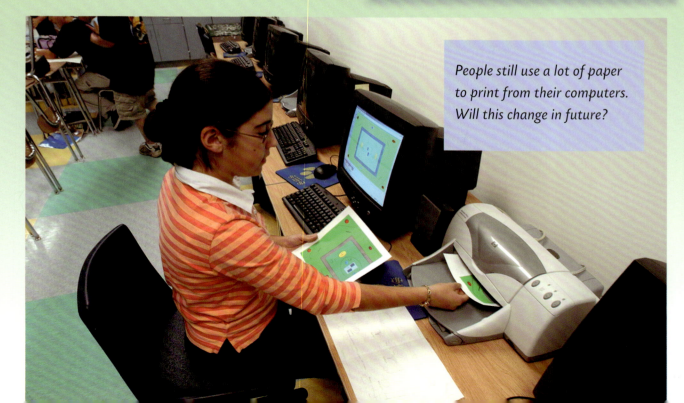

People still use a lot of paper to print from their computers. Will this change in future?

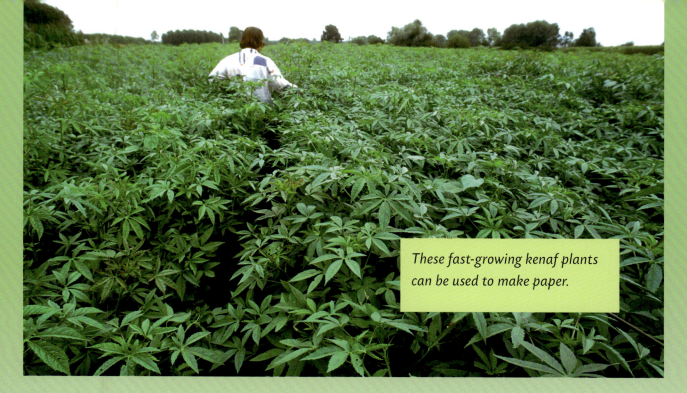

These fast-growing kenaf plants can be used to make paper.

Paper from plants

The kenaf plant is similar to hemp and jute. It can grow to five metres tall in just a few months. Traditionally people have made rope, twine and coarse cloth from kenaf fibre, but recently it has been used to make paper. Experts believe that we could grow kenaf specially to make paper, as it is easier to grow and grows more quickly than trees. One hectare of kenaf can produce about 20 tonnes of fibre for making paper in one season. The same area of pine forest produces about six tonnes of fibre. Kenaf pulp is also whiter than wood pulp.

Will there be enough wood?

We will probably need more and more wood for pulp in the next 50 years, but experts think that we do produce enough wood fibre at present. They calculate that the pulpwood we need could come from a plantation about 400,000 square kilometres in size.

This is an area slightly larger than Norway or slightly smaller than the US state of California.

RECYCLE RECYCLE RECYCLE

MORE HELP FOR THE ENVIRONMENT

Today's environmental campaigners have some key aims for papermakers. They want:
• more recycled pulp used to make paper;
• people to use less paper and recycle more of what they use;
• specially appointed organizations to look after forests;
• stricter rules about how we use land so forests are not turned into paper plantations;
• no more chemicals used to bleach paper.

Glossary

beater house   A place in old paper mills where rags were beaten to make pulp.

biofuel   A fuel produced from biomass (plant or animal matter).

bleach   A substance used to whiten paper.

Buddhist   Related to Buddhism, a religion and philosophy founded in ancient India.

carbohydrate   A substance made up of carbon, hydrogen and oxygen. Sugar, starch and cellulose are carbohydrates.

carbon   A non-metallic chemical element in coal and many other substances.

cellulose   A substance that makes up the cell walls of plants.

coniferous trees   Cone-bearing, needle-leaved trees, such as fir, pine and spruce. Most conifers are evergreen and do not drop their leaves in autumn.

corrugated   Folded in ridges and grooves.

crusade   One of a series of holy wars in the Middle Ages. European Christian knights wanted to capture land in the Middle East from Muslim forces.

deckle   A flat metal frame that holds wet pulp during papermaking.

digester   A large tank in which substances are broken down by chemicals.

environmentalist   A person who looks after the natural environment.

esparto grass   A tough kind of grass with narrow leaves.

fibres   Tiny, thread-like plant cells.

flexible   Able to bend easily.

found objects   Things that artists find and use in their work, such as pieces of paper, metal or cloth.

graphic design   The art of combining printed words and pictures, especially in books and magazines.

greenhouse effect   Warming of the Earth's surface caused especially by pollution from burning fossil fuels (coal, gas and oil).

hardwood   The kind of wood that comes from broadleaved trees, such as birch or oak.

hectare   A unit of area the same as 10,000 square metres.

hemp   A woody plant that can be used for making paper and rope.

hydrogen   A light, colourless gas that combines with oxygen to make water.

jute   A tropical plant with tough fibres.

kilowatt hours (kWh)   An amount of electrical energy (the same as 1000 watts) used in one hour.

lignin   A substance that holds plant fibres together and makes plants rigid and woody.

lithography   A printing process using a flat surface (or plate) on which words and pictures take up greasy ink that can be pressed on to paper.

megajoules   A unit of energy (one million joules).

mould   A hollow container that shapes a wet or molten substance when it hardens.

oxygen   A colourless gas that humans and animals need to breathe to live.

pollution Damage to the environment caused by harmful substances.

pulp A wet, slushy mass of fibres that is used to make paper.

resin A sticky substance produced by some plants.

saliva Watery liquid produced in the mouth; spit.

shock absorber Something that takes in (or absorbs) jolts and knocks, to protect something else from damage.

sodium hydroxide A burning substance that is used in making paper, soap and other materials; also called caustic soda.

sodium sulphide A substance used to break down wood fibres and make pulp.

softwood The kind of wood that comes from coniferous trees, such as fir or pine.

stamper A heavy wooden hammer used in paper mills to beat rags and make pulp.

starch A white substance from plants that can be used to stiffen things.

sulphate A chemical substance that contains the elements sulphur and oxygen.

typography The art and process of arranging letters and words to be printed.

vellum Parchment (a flat material for writing on) made from calfskin.

Websites

The Story of Paper-Making: written for the J.W. Butler Paper Company in 1901.
www.aboutbookbinding.com/Paper/PaperMaking-Main.html

Information on the Paper Trail project, an old paper mill in southern England.
www.thepapertrail.org.uk

A diagram showing the parts of a Fourdrinier papermaking machine.
www.hertfordshire-genealogy.co.uk/data/topics/t093-paper-makers-apsley.htm

Fact sheets from the Confederation of Paper Industries and the Paper Industries Technical Association.
www.paper.org.uk/information/pages/fact_sheets.html
http://pita.co.uk/factsheets/

Interesting facts about paper and recycling from the US Paper University.
www.tappi.org/paperu/all_about_paper/earth_answers/earthAnswers.htm

Articles from the Ecology Global Network on papermaking and the environment.
www.ecology.com/features/paperchase/index.html

Index